Contents

Feeling angry!

Everybody feels angry sometimes. You might feel angry if...

...somebody does something that upsets you.

...you feel that something unfair has happened.

ANGRY!

...you're told you can't do something you really want to do.

...something you own gets messed up.

...you get blamed for something that wasn't your fault.

Everybody Feels...
ANGRY!

Moira Butterfield
& Holly Sterling

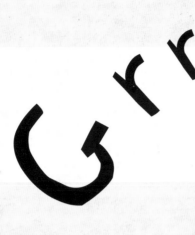

Grrr!

Quarto is the authority on a wide range of topics.

Quarto educates, entertains and enriches the lives of
our readers—enthusiasts and lovers of hands-on living.
www.quartoknows.com

Consultant: Cecilia Essau
Design: Barbi Sido, Mike Henson
Editor: Carly Madden
Editorial Director: Victoria Garrard
Art Director: Laura Roberts-Jensen
Associate Publisher: Maxime Boucknooghe
Publisher: Zeta Jones

First published in the UK in hardcover in 2016 by
QED Publishing
Part of The Quarto Group
The Old Brewery
6 Blundell Street
London N7 9BH

A catalogue record for this book is
available from the British Library.

ISBN 978 1 78493 855 0

Printed in China

How it feels

It happens quickly,

before you can think.

The angry feeling comes rushing in.

Your face screws up.

Your fists squeeze up.

You open your mouth

and...

SHOUT!

Angry girl

Hello. I'm Sophie. Yesterday I was busy colouring a really good picture when I saw our dog, Meg, chewing my trainer.

NOOO!

When I went to stop Meg, my little brother Oscar drew on my picture.

Straight away I filled up
with angry feelings. I felt
like a kettle about to boil.

GRRRRR!

I screwed up my face...

...I bunched up
my fists and...

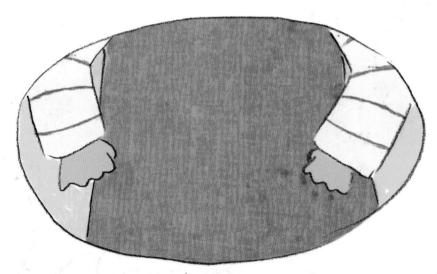

BAM!

I turned into Angry Girl.

"Stop it,"
I shouted.

I sounded as loud
as a roaring lion!

I was so loud
that Oscar
cried and
Meg hid under
the table.

10

Angry boy

Hello. My name's Ethan. Yesterday Gran gave me a chocolate bar.

Thanks, Gran!

I put it in the kitchen cupboard ready to eat when I was hungry.

12

When **I** went to get the **chocolate** later...

...it was gone!

Then I found the empty wrapper on the table.

Someone had eaten **my treat.**

I began to fill up with angry feelings.

I felt like a balloon about to burst...

Agggh!

Then my brother Jack came in, and **I** saw chocolate round his mouth.

POP!
I turned into
Angry Boy!

It's
not
fair!

"You ate my chocolate!
You're **horrible!**"
I shouted and I ran outside.

17

Feeling better

Ethan saw Sophie next door.
She was **unhappy** too.
He went round to her garden where it was calm
and quiet. Talking about how they felt made
them both **feel better**.

Oscar said sorry to Sophie
and they made friends.

Jack said sorry, too.
He gave Ethan another
chocolate bar.

Angry Girl and Angry Boy had gone!

Sophie's story

1 Sophie got angry with Oscar and Meg for what they did.

2 Then she had some quiet time and it helped her to calm down.

3 It helped to talk to somebody about her feelings.

4 She made friends with Oscar and Meg again, and she felt lots better.

Ethan's story

1 Ethan got angry with Jack for eating his chocolate bar.

2 Talking to Sophie helped him to feel better.

3 Having some quiet time helped him to feel calm, too.

4 Jack said sorry and he and Ethan made friends again. Ethan stopped feeling angry.

Story words

blamed

When somebody thinks you did something wrong. Ethan blamed Jack for eating his chocolate.

boil

To bubble up like hot water in a kettle. Sophie felt like that when she got angry.

bunched

When something squeezes tight. Sophie bunched up her fists when she felt angry.

burst

When something pops apart, like a balloon bursting. Ethan felt like a balloon about to burst when he got angry.

POP!

calm

When you feel happy and not upset about anything. It's as if your feelings go quiet.

quiet time

A little bit of time spent somewhere quiet.

saying sorry

Telling someone you didn't mean to upset them. It's good to say sorry if you have made someone feel angry.

shouting

Sometimes we can't help shouting when we feel angry. It's as if the angry feelings come rushing out of our mouths!

stomping

Banging your feet on the ground as you walk along. You might feel like stomping if you are angry.

talking

Telling somebody something. It can make you feel less angry if you talk to someone about how you feel.

treat

Something good. Jack ate Ethan's treat, the bar of chocolate.

unfair

When something that doesn't seem right happens to someone. When Jack ate Ethan's chocolate it was unfair.

23

Next steps

The stories in this book have been written to give children an introduction to feeling angry through events that they are familiar with. Here are some ideas to help you explore the feelings from the story together.

Talking

- Look at Sophie and Ethan's stories. Talk about what made them both feel angry. Can your child remember a time when they felt angry? How did their body show them they were angry?

- Both Sophie and Ethan shouted when they became angry. Ask your child to describe how shouting makes them feel. How do they feel when somebody shouts at them?
- Discuss how Sophie and Ethan stopped feeling angry. Talk about when it's good to say sorry.
- Look at the poem on page 5 and talk to your child about how they feel when they are angry. You could help them write a poem themselves.
- Everybody is angry sometimes. Talk to your child about when being angry might be the right way to feel.

Make up a story

On pages 20–21 the stories have been broken down into four-stage sequences. Use this as a model to work together, making a simple sequence of events about somebody getting angry and then calming down. Ask your child to suggest the sequence of events and a way to resolve their story at the end.

An art session

Do a drawing session related to the feeling in this book. Here are some suggestions for drawings:

- Someone who is so angry they feel like a balloon about to burst.
- Someone who is so angry they roar like a lion.
- People making friends after being angry.

An acting session

Choose a scene and act it out, for example:

- Role-play Sophie and Oscar (who draws on her picture when she is not looking). Act out Sophie calming down, talking to Ethan and making friends with Oscar again.
- Role-play Ethan and Jack (who takes Ethan's chocolate). Show Ethan calming down, talking to Sophie and making friends with Jack again.